THE SIMPLE (NOT EASY) GUIDE TO WIN IN REAL ESTATE

BRYAN CASELLA

Copyright © 2026 Bryan Casella

All rights reserved. No part of this publication may be reproduced, distributed, or transmitted in any form or by any means, including photocopying, recording, or other electronic or mechanical methods, without the prior written permission of the publisher, except in the case of brief quotations embodied in critical reviews and certain other noncommercial uses permitted by copyright law.

ISBN: 979-8-9910103-5-1

First printing edition 2026

Printed by Domor Books in the United States of America.

TABLE OF CONTENTS

INTRODUCTION

Eventually, everyone reaches a point where it dawns on them that they are not the same as everyone else. When you reach that point, you question what everyone else willingly goes along with, and you know in your heart of hearts that you will never live as other people do.

You will walk your own path and live by your own rules.

You are not bound and confined to the same physical and mental prison that others are stuck in.

You refuse to accept their opinions and limitations.

You want and desire more for yourself and your future.

You may not know the reason or how, but that seed is within you.

Now it's just a matter of watering it, feeding it, and watching it blossom into a force to be reckoned with.

I knew from a young age that I would be famous (whatever that means). More specifically, I knew that many people would know my name. It wouldn't be because I was special; it would be because I had earned it.

I had visions at that time of playing in packed stadiums. I could clearly envision myself wearing a jersey with my last name on the back, hearing the roar of the crowd as I performed. It was clear to me then that I wasn't going to live a normal life.

I went to college on an athletic scholarship, and part of the terms was the work study program. This program required me to work an on-campus job during the school year. Failure to do so would cause me to lose my scholarship.

I chose to work at the student library (one of the few choices we had for work study) and remember showing up on day one, kind of excited and not sure what to expect. Immediately, I began to notice a clear difference between me and everyone else who was working there. Regardless of what it was, I worked diligently and with pride. I showed up early, stayed late, and did the best job that I could. I went above and beyond what was required of me. The other students were the opposite: always complaining, showing up late, leaving early, and doing the bare minimum amount of work.

Eventually, it got to the point where I was getting upset, and I approached the faculty, making it known to them that I was working extra hard and that the other students weren't doing their jobs. I requested to be paid more or for those students to be let go. Long story short, nothing happened. Emails were sent, notes were passed, and I was continuously blown off.

This was my first "real" experience of what we label as "Corporate America," even though it wasn't some big-ticket type of job or career. I knew from that moment at 19 years old that, regardless of what my future held, I would do my best to never work for someone else again and subjugate myself to those circumstances! This, unbeknownst to me at the time, would prove to be a significant decision and commitment later in my future.

YOU HAVE TO BE IN THE BUSINESS OF PEOPLE

My family originates from Argentina. My parents, my two older brothers, and everyone else in my family were born and raised in South America. I am the first in my bloodline to be born on American soil. I only knew Spanish when I went to school, and learned English officially as my second language. My family roots are simple. Humble, hard-working, poor people doing what they can to have enough money to pay for food and rent. No fancy things, no rich uncle, and nothing that someone could say, "Wow, you hit the genetic lottery."

Let's talk about real estate and being a realtor. What you and the public see and believe about the profession is full of misconceptions and distorted facts. The fancy suits, calls to "negotiate" million-dollar deals, the fast cars, the parties, and all the rest of it are fake. Reality television and the internet have created an alternate reality that people think is real. Newsflash, the world you see and interact with off your phone is reality, not what's on your screen.

Why am I saying this? Because just as Bruce Lee said, "I want you to empty your mind...be formless, shapeless like water." I would like you to read and understand the words in this book as if you were a brand-new student showing up on day one, ready and hungry to learn EVERYTHING. I am going to challenge you, upset you, anger you, scare you, and much, much more. This isn't for the dabblers and faint of heart.

Being a realtor today has become like a meme, almost like how everyone who claims to be an actor. It has become so far detached from the traditional business practices and principles that people forget it is a real business. The TikTokers and gurus have led most people astray. Fortunately for you, I am going to bring you back into reality!

There is no doubt that technology, our economy, and the modern world have brought some changes to the business of real estate. However, fundamentally, it remains the same. This is a people business! Yes, a people business. Meaning you will have to engage with, talk to, befriend, sell to, host, negotiate, work with, and build relationships with many people. This is the fundamental law in entrepreneurship and operates independently of anything we say, what our opinions are, our personalities, etc. It's just a fact! We cannot change or avoid it. You get with the program, or you fade away into obscurity.

All I see nowadays are strategies, marketing, and conversations around everything but that. Excuses, stories, and everything else about why someone doesn't want to do the "old school" or "hard" work and just wants to work less and make money hand over fist. If that's you, turn in your license and go get a 9-5 job. You have no business being an entrepreneur.

The first step is to accept the fact that you're going to have to talk to a lot of people every...single...day! From a social standpoint, we have gone so far backwards as a society that it feels overwhelming to most people. If you have little to no business, are new, or just flat out want to be a rockstar in the industry, I'd recommend you speak to at least 40-50 people daily regarding real estate. To be clear, SPEAK to...not email, not direct message, not send videos to—I mean live conversations. This is a monumental task for most agents and entrepreneurs for one reason and one reason alone—our insecurities.

Talking to people is easy. We complicate it and make it hard. We fear rejection, think we're ugly, hate the sound of our own voice, know we need to lose weight, and I can go on and on and on...so you're faced with a tough decision. Will you take massive action despite this, or will you keep riding the train of mediocrity and misery? You must become sick of your sickness and have the desire to change! No one can help you with that or convince you that it is 100% your decision and your responsibility. You either want to change and evolve or you don't, plain and simple. If you don't, then hang it up and stop making excuses and complaining. If you do, then get to work and make it happen.

Here is a simple list of things you can do to talk to 40-50 people a day:

- Cold call
- Door knock
- Preview knock
- Seller seminars
- Old FSBO
- Expired FSBO
- Just listed/just sold
- Farming
- SOI events
- Meet up groups
- Networking
- Open houses
- Buyer seminars
- Interview local businesses

YOU CAN'T BE AFRAID OF HARD WORK

When I started 13 years ago in 2013, I knew I was going to have to do everything differently, things I had never done before. It was scary and intense; however, I embraced it. I kept it simple: knock on 100 doors a day and make 200 calls a day. I usually made 25-30 contacts by knocking and had an average answer rate of 5% on calls. My commitment was 50 new contacts a day. Not my goal—my commitment. This is what my schedule was for my first 3 years in the business before I built my team and grew into what you see today.

5 am - Wake up
5:15-6:15 am - Gym
6:30-7:15 am - Read
7:30-8:00 am - Roleplay
8 am-noon - Prospecting
Noon-1 pm - Lunch break
1-2 pm - Follow Up
2-3:30 pm - More Roleplay
3:30-4 pm - Education/Admin
4-6 pm - Appointments/Prospecting

That was it. It was as simple as that. A full-time realtor putting in a full day's worth of work. I did this basically 6 days a week, sometimes 7. There is no doubt in my mind that if anyone followed this schedule 100% for 90-120 days, they would have an explosion of leads, appointments, and deals.

Let's be real, though, because I've talked about this schedule and activities for over 12 years now, and maybe a handful (if that) of people have actually followed it and stuck with it. I'd recommend you follow this 80% of the time. Is it easy? Nope. Is it sexy? Nope. However, it gets results! This is how you build a business from the ground up. Not all that nonsense marketers feed you to fatten their pockets and keep you stuck with no results.

Start calling people you know, start knocking on doors around where you live, start chatting up managers and employees of businesses you frequent, start hosting meetups, start going live on your platforms. Get out there and start talking to a lot of people every day about real estate. You'll be surprised how quickly it becomes automatic, and you'll start to build momentum.

What a lot of people either don't know or forget is that when you're not good at something, it sucks—it's hard, not fun, difficult, and frustrating. Eventually, you get better, and later you'll get really good. Then you start looking forward to the activity, have fun, bend the rules, and start getting some very good results.

This is the key, and what everyone has to understand—practice makes perfect. The best part is that real estate is a sales business. It's a communication game. The study, understanding, and application of communication is a science. Anyone can learn it. I don't care what you think or what people say. You—yes, you the reader—can be just as good a communicator as I am or even better.

The question is, are you willing to do what I did to get there? Would you be willing to learn from me? If your answers are yes, then it is accessible to you. This isn't a sport where genetics give certain people an unfair advantage. In this communication game, we're all in the same boat, and the ones who are at the top are the ones who study and apply what they've learned the most!

I know that most people reading this aren't used to direct, clear, and brutally honest communication. The voice in their heads has probably been going on and on, potentially dismissing what I've said and already making up more excuses and stories that this won't work or it's "too extreme." Those voices aren't you. You're hearing society, doubters, and all the false conditioning you've accumulated and carry with you daily that simply weigh you down and keep you docile. The immediate solution to that is massive action. When you're moving, you do not give your mind and these voices any time to bother you. When you sit still and do nothing, the demons come out.

So where do we start? How do we get all this going? Simple. I will give you a set of tasks to get you started.

STEP 1

PREPARE YOUR PEOPLE

First, I want you to sit down with your family, spouse, kids, parents, and anyone else who is important to you and with whom you have frequent and close contact. Next, I want you to share your goals and commitments with them. Share that schedule I gave you with them and ask them to respect and honor it. Let them know you may be unavailable during your work hours. Ask those around you to accept the fact that you are going for it and you are 100% committed.

Now, they may not respect this or take you seriously, but that's ok. You honor your side of this commitment. I also want you to post these commitments on your social media (and tag me if you're bold enough!) Most people never take this first step, and that is one of the many reasons they crack under pressure and start self-sabotaging. Remember, nobody owes you anything! (and vice versa.)

STEP 2

CONTACT EVERYONE

Second, I want you to start making a list of everyone you know... EVERYONE. Cell phone, email, and address. When I started, this list was about 45-50 people. Take the time and do it because this is the beginning of your sphere of influence list. We will be adding to and expanding on this later.

STEP 3

DRESS TO IMPRESS

Go into your closet and pull out your professional clothes. Fellas and ladies, all you need are two suits and about 3-4 different shirts and ties to go with them. Keep it simple. If you don't have a pair of dress shoes, grab some cheap ones because you're going to be hitting doors, and you don't want to tear your feet apart.

This is where we have to start thinking about strategy. When someone knocks on your door, how are they dressed? Typically, a generic polo shirt or a generic suit. Do your best to avoid generic black/grey suits with the white dress shirt. Even if it's not your "style," get some shirts and ties that pop! This will work wonders in getting more doors to open and having people respond to you differently. The intention behind this is so that people don't automatically categorize you as someone not worth talking to or identify you as someone that you're not.

STEP 4
FIGURE OUT YOUR FUTURE

Fourth, I want you to become crystal clear about who you want to become and where you want to be in the future. Not what mom and dad expect from you. Not what you think you need to be. I mean what you truly desire. Most people go around living other people's lives, not their own. Their goals, careers, and interests aren't theirs. They're someone else's! This is why most of the planet is unmotivated, lost, disinterested, and apathetic. This disconnect is like a plague on this planet.

Now, this process can take time. However, you don't pause life and wait to figure this out. You practice awareness (being in the moment) and take massive action. This will open the floodgates and provide you with an experience you've never had before.

STEP 5

TAKE MASSIVE ACTION

I want you to accept right now that you don't have all the answers. Repeat this again and again. I am ok not knowing everything—I will still work hard every single day! Most people make excuses and say they have to "figure it all out before they start." Nonsense! The time to start is now, and the best way to learn is through experience and expert guidance. You gain experience through action, and then you have the expert (coach) to help guide you as you go. You must take massive action every day for your business to grow and to improve your life. No excuse or story is valid! This is the path of excellence, and I invite you to join us.

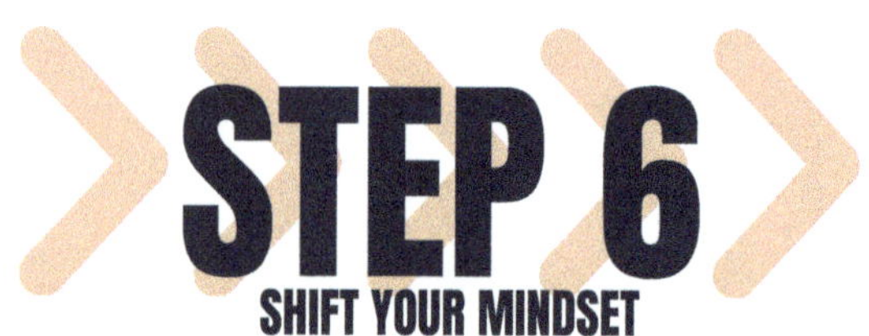

STEP 6
SHIFT YOUR MINDSET

Sixth, I want you to understand now that you must make a fundamental shift in your mindset. You're a CEO now, not an employee.

You don't clock in and out.

You work until the job is done.

You don't take weekends off—you use them to get ahead like any other workday.

You don't get paid every 2 weeks. You get paid when you produce.

You don't get in trouble for being late or not working hard...you simply fail out of the business.

Hopefully I've made my point. It's on YOU! You must take full responsibility for yourself and your business.

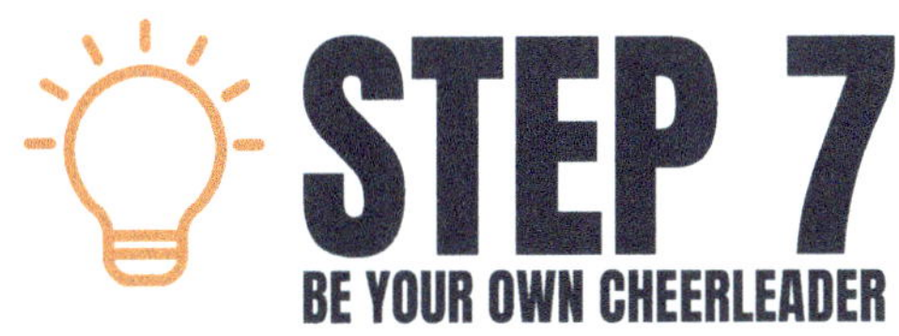

STEP 7

BE YOUR OWN CHEERLEADER

Seven is a tough one, and most people struggle with this point. I learned this lesson early on in life. Accept and be ok with the fact that no one except you has to support your goals and dreams.

I still get messages daily like, "Hey Bryan, how do I get my parents to accept and support my goals?" The simple answer is you can't. Anyone else's support and cheering are a bonus, not a requirement. It's a tough pill to swallow, but it is a reality we must all accept. The good news is you'll find others and get around other people like you (which I'll touch on later). Full acceptance of this point and getting over the emotions of it requires you to put your big boy/big girl pants on and step into your bad-ass mode.

Remember that this path of entrepreneurship requires you to operate the opposite of most people. You have to be "crazy." When you realize and understand that, things like this become much easier to accept and adopt into your life.

STEP 8

LEAVE THE OLD YOU BEHIND

The new you begins today, and with this decision, a paradigm shift occurs, and your old reality will shatter into pieces. This is scary, but it's a requirement for growth and success. The old you must be left behind, and you must now create the new you. Take stock of your thoughts, ideas, actions, friends, habits, hobbies, vices, addictions, beliefs, philosophies. All of them will have to be analyzed deeply and changed. What doesn't serve you will have to be left behind and replaced with what does serve you. Most people fail at this point because they are unwilling to leave behind what keeps them trapped instead of being committed to their future self. They instead choose comfortable misery.

STEP 9

GET ACCOUNTABILITY

Intense accountability is something else you will need, but most people are allergic to it. There are two components: internal and external accountability. Internal accountability is obviously the most important of the two. When your workout partner misses or flakes out, do you still go to the gym and hit it hard? This internal accountability must be built and strengthened by you daily. Doing the little things—following your schedule, waking up on time, starting your calls at exactly 8 am every morning—are all examples of ways to develop this "muscle."

External accountability will require you to put yourself in a position where you force yourself to do things, and others keep you in check. Combining both is the recipe for success in any endeavor. Whatever it takes, both are required to get to the highest levels and maximize your individual potential.

Tenth, commit to understanding human nature and communication. We are bombarded daily with videos, podcasts, and free media. Although they are nice to have, they by no means are the path to mastery. I remember being a brand-new real estate agent and going to my first event (even before I was licensed). I did whatever I had to do to get around the top dogs. I asked about 100 top agents to roleplay scripts with me, and four said yes. All were top-producing agents. I signed up for coaching at that first event too, because even though I didn't have the money and had every excuse in the book not to, I knew it would be necessary if I wanted to succeed at the highest levels. I idolized Kobe Bryant growing up, and he had over ten coaches in his life at one time! Emulate the best if you want to be the best!

Additionally, in the rapidly shifting digital world, people are becoming more and more hesitant and skeptical. In order to thrive in this kind of environment, you must have an elite skillset in communication and sales to effectively contact, capture, and convert customers. This skillset will serve you equally in the real world and online.

STEP 11

FOCUS ON PROGRESS

Eleventh, become obsessed not with results but with progress! Record your calls, listing presentations, roleplay sessions, and send them to your coach for comment and critique! Record yourself on your phone reciting all your scripts with perfect delivery and play it in your car every single day. Spend at least two hours a day practicing and roleplaying dialogues. Get certified in NLP and Hypnotherapy. Read all the books I've recommended on my YouTube channel over the years. This absolute dedication to getting better is what gets you results. Focus on the activities and things that create a better version of you that will capture more business and allow you to be more successful.

STEP 12

TRACK EVERYTHING

Track your numbers. In fact, track everything! Contacts, leads, appointments, lead sources, time worked, listings taken, buyers under contract, etc. Track your numbers every single workday. When you do a business review and sit down with your coach, this is the main metric we will look at to spot strengths, weaknesses, and adjustments that need to be made. No numbers = no business. Nine out of ten realtors will never consistently track their numbers, and it's one of the many reasons they fail. You can spot patterns, and those adjustments are the difference.

STEP 13

PUSH YOUR LIMITS

I want you to focus daily on stretching your limits and boundarie What does that mean? Well, if posting your opinion on Faceboo about something makes you scared, POST IT RIGHT NOW! You w have to commit to continuously pushing past your boundaries an limitations. Eventually, you stretch so far that your everyday lif becomes effortless.

I've done improv (comedy), I've gone alone to nightclubs, I'v approached strangers on the street...I've done all that and more in th spirit of shattering all barriers and limitations. If this becomes standard and focus in your life, you will evolve rapidly.

STEP 14

DON'T SEEK APPROVAL

Release your addiction to approval. So much of what we do (witho realizing it) is approval seeking. Being overly nice, hesitating to say do something, posting for likes and attention, feeling like you "nee to party—the list goes on and on. This one takes a lot of time and r programming. However, it absolutely must be a top priority. Are y living your life? Or are you trying to live based on someone els expectations? A lack of motivation, drive, and focus is often caus by this one issue. Get clear with yourself and begin to purge th sickness immediately.

DO NOT, and I repeat DO NOT, allow yourself to fall for this one thing. Look, times will be tough, and we will all eventually have moments of weakness. There are so many "new" methods, "cheat codes," and other magic bullets that will be thrown in your face. Pay them no mind. Immediately unfollow most content creators, leave most Facebook groups, and funnel your attention to your strategy, your coach, and your community. Everything else is a distraction! This will simplify the journey for you and eliminate most distractions. If this means that you unfollow me, then so be it. Until you master your initial systems and processes, you don't want anything else to confuse you.

The issue today for most agents is that they follow 1,000 people who give them 1,000 different ideas, which they try to mash together to create their own "system." This never works. Master one methodology and system before doing anything else or adding anything new.

STEP 16

STAY HEALTHY

Prioritize your health and wellness. Get to sleep early, wake up early, eat clean, avoid alcohol, smoking, pills, energy drinks, coffee, stay off your phone, limit TV and app usage, get some sun, breathe fresh air, exercise, and move your body. This will elevate your mood, give you abundant energy, improve your sleep, make you calmer and more relaxed, and ultimately allow you to make it through the "grind" a little easier. This one is "obvious," but most people neglect it entirely. This has been one of the foundational principles that has allowed me to stay so consistent and grounded over the last 10-12 years.

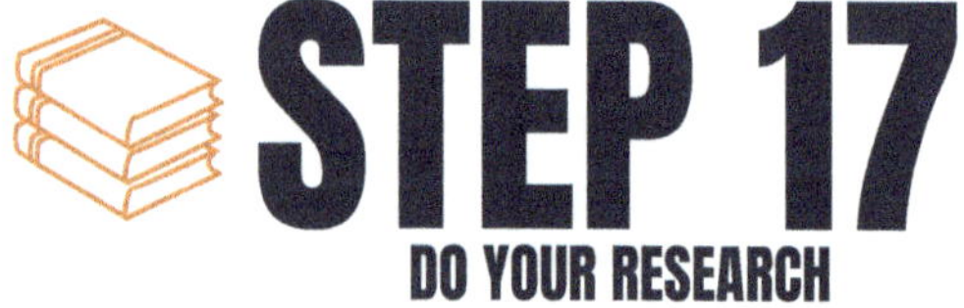

STEP 17

DO YOUR RESEARCH

Get back to non-digital education. Attend in-person lectures and read physical books. Nothing beats that. Put down the phone, iPad, and earbuds, get a pen, paper, and a good book. Read, take notes, and really connect with your studies.

STEP 18

PLAN YOUR TRANSITION

Staying afloat when you start is the most challenging thing you'll face. You have two options—transition from your part-time/full-time job in 6-12 months to full-time real estate, or get a side hustle while you're full-time in real estate.

LET'S TALK ABOUT SOCIAL MEDIA

Now, since I know we're in the modern era and everyone is so focused on social media/technology, let's talk about it. Think of social media and tech as a way to enhance your efforts. The systems and software we use (for lead gen, CRMs, etc.), social media for free marketing, and having access to the world at our fingertips are great. Video marketing is obviously huge, and how most of you likely came across me.
Tech makes our jobs way easier. Here are some great tools:

1. Enzo/Batch/Call Tools/Mojo Dialer - Multi-line dialers you can use
2. Vulcan7/Cole Realty Resource/Haines directory/Propstream - Data for leads to call/contact
3. Lofty/Top Producer/Kvcore/Go High Level - CRM software for your database
4. Bomb Bomb/Mail Chimp/Constant Contact - Email software for drips (if your CRM doesn't include it)

Nowadays, you also have tons of apps for virtually all of your business needs. Some of these that I've listed above are great to get you started and will lay the foundation for you to grow from.

Share your journey on social media from the get-go. I built one of the largest brands in this industry by starting as a complete nobody, sharing my journey with the world. Keep it simple. Show clips of you calling, door knocking, doing showings, your morning routine, and all of your business activities.

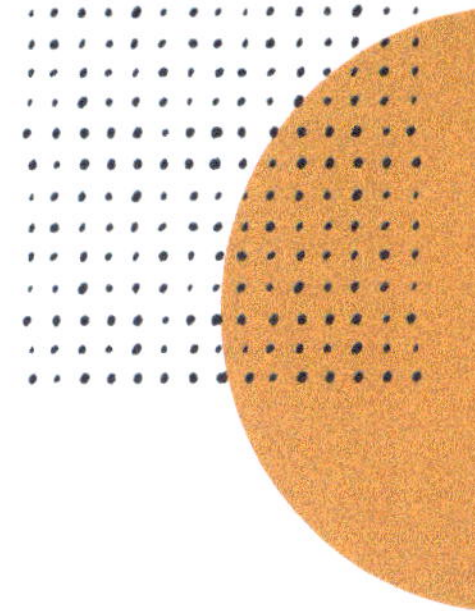

The biggest piece to the puzzle that must be present in your content is authenticity. Love me or hate me, I am who I am. You know exactly what I'm about. I've met and worked with so many "influencers" in our industry, and a lot of them are fake. You would be shocked if you saw who they really are and how they talk about people. Many are liars who are being two-faced. Remember that people can see through that, and eventually the truth will come out. All the people who used to attack me back in 2018...where are they now? Honesty, transparency, and authenticity need to be the foundation of your brand.

People saw themselves in me and could relate to what I was sharing. When people can see you as a colleague and friend, the trust gap is filled, and now you have a true follower and supporter.

Building from a simple, proper foundation allows you to grow and flourish correctly. Seeing and growing something you enjoy and are excited about is what will carry you. I took pride in what I was putting out and enjoyed documenting the process. I looked forward to sharing and was excited to capture moments and put ideas on paper. Content creation became a form of personal journaling and expression for me.

Bottom line: keep it simple and post! Here are a few ideas and topics for creating content:

1. Current events/industry news
2. Special moments
3. Learning lessons
4. Expectations vs. reality
5. Day in the life
6. Live calls/action
7. Goals and commitments
8. Funny takes/moments
9. Gratitude/appreciation
10. Client wins/stories
11. Accomplishments
12. Vulnerability

It's a damn shame that censorship got my previous platforms removed and deleted, otherwise I'd direct you to them to get those older, specific examples. Remember, consistency is king and the most important thing long-term.

I'm keeping this first book as minimalist and simple as possible for a few key reasons. Firstly, I want you to get to work, as that is by far the most important thing. Secondly, we all know that too much information is one of the biggest problems at the moment and is yet another reason why so many people are failing. Lastly, to demonstrate to you that massive success really is that simple. Not easy, but simple.

Now that we're in the modern era, the people who dominate in our industry will be those who master both sides of the business—the traditional methods and the "new" school. I truly believe I am one of the original people who showed the world how to do that and achieved massive success from it. (My peak year was $1.6 million in revenue.) If you learn and master the fundamental principles of this business and then embrace the new school things, you will absolutely rise to the top.

GET SOMEONE IN YOUR CORNER

The last thing I'll leave you with is GET A COACH! I got one before I was officially licensed, and it was the best decision I ever made. I wanted to start correctly and make sure that I set myself up for success from day one. YouTube, books, and podcasts will never replace being personally helped by an expert. With coaching, you'll be getting the magical 3 S's that you need. Skills, Systems, and Support.

Skills teach you communication techniques, sales skills, content creation, follow-up, presentations, scripts, and all the other essential things you need.

Systems will teach you the Standard Operating Procedures (SOP), database, CRM, follow-up structure, workflows, email campaigns, marketing, events, and all other essential structures to make you a legitimate business owner.

Lastly, we have support from both your coach and community. This is extremely overlooked and has become one of the most important pillars. Having real accountability partners, live calls/calling sessions, and a place to get your questions answered is the exact thing you need to keep you locked in and focused.

IT'S ALL ABOUT PERSONAL DEVELOPMENT

The final note I'll add about this is yet another thing no one really talks about, and that is a real mindset for personal development. At the end of the day, you can have the 3 S's, but if you're ill-equipped in the personal development side, you will fail. I will argue that most realtors fail because of this. You know what to do, but you simply do not do it at all or not consistently enough.

This is why my coaching and training platform covers this extensively. If you do not change and grow internally as a person, your success (or lack thereof) will reflect that. We do one live lecture per week and two mini mastermind calls, and also an optional Toastmasters (public speaking) call. I won't turn this into a sales pitch, so contact me privately on social or go to www.BryanCasella.com for more info.

Now, it's time to get to work! You have everything you need here to get started and build your business. This year, I'm personally focusing on continuing to build Team BC, my nationwide real estate team, my coaching platforms, my new social media accounts, and lastly, my network at Real Brokerage! Best wishes to you!

Think real estate is about flashy deals and easy money? Think again.

In this direct, no-excuses guide, Bryan Casella reveals what it really takes to succeed: relentless work, real conversations, and total ownership of your life and business. From daily prospecting to mastering communication, he lays out the simple —but not easy—formula for building momentum and closing deals.

This isn't for dabblers. It's for those ready to take massive action and become unstoppable.

Bryan Casella is a real estate entrepreneur, coach, and content creator known for his no-nonsense approach. He built his business from the ground up through discipline, prospecting, and mastering communication, and now trains agents nationwide to do the same.

www.ingramcontent.com/pod-product-compliance
Ingram Content Group UK Ltd.
Pitfield, Milton Keynes, MK11 3LW, UK
UKHW062253290726
14090UKWH00017B/657

9 798991 010351